D0128652

# Quick Tropical Throw

DESIGN BY MELISSA LEAPMAN

## EXPERIENCE LEVEL

**EASY**

## FINISHED SIZE

Approx 43 x 48 inches

## MATERIALS

- Mercerized worsted weight cotton yarn (77 yds/1¾ oz per ball): 10 balls white (A); 13 balls each bright yellow (B), orange (C), lime (D)
- Size 10 (6mm) circular needle
- Size 11 (8mm) circular needle or size needed to obtain gauge

## GAUGE

10 sts and 16 rows = 4 inches/10cm with larger needle and 3 strands of yarn held tog
To save time, take time to check gauge.

## PATTERN NOTES

Project uses 3 strands of yarn held tog throughout.

Circular needles are used to accommodate the large number of sts; do not join at end of rows.

Border is worked with A throughout.

## THROW

With smaller needle and 3 strands of A held tog, cast on 109 sts. Work 10 rows of garter st.

Change to larger needle and beg main pat:

**Rows 1 and 3 (RS):** With A, k5; with B, knit across to last 5 sts; with 2nd ball of A, k5.

**Rows 2 and 4:** With A, k5; with B, purl across to last 5 sts; with 2nd ball of A, k5.

**Row 5:** With A, k5; with C, *k3, insert RH needle into st 4 rows below next st on needle and pull up a lp, knit next st, then pass lp over knitted st, rep from * across to last 8 sts, end k3; with 2nd ball of A, k5.

**Rows 6 and 8:** Rep Rows 2 and 4, using C instead of B.

**Row 7:** Rep Row 1, using C instead of B.

**Row 9:** With A, k5; with D, k1, *insert RH needle into st 4 rows below next st on needle and pull up a lp, knit next st, then pass lp over knitted st, k3, rep from * across to last 7 sts, end insert RH needle into st 4 rows below next st on needle and pull up a lp, knit next st, then pass lp over knitted st, k1; with 2nd ball of A, k5.

**Rows 10 and 12:** Rep Rows 2 and 4, using D instead of B.

**Row 11:** Rep Row 1, using D instead of B.

**Row 13:** Rep Row 5, using B instead of D.

**Row 14 and 16:** Rep Rows 2 and 4, using B instead of D.

**Row 15:** Rep Row 1, using B instead of D.

**Row 17:** Rep Row 9, using C instead of B.

**Rows 18 and 20:** Rep Rows 2 and 4, using C instead of B.

**Row 19:** Rep Row 1, using C instead of B.

**Row 21:** Rep Row 5, using D instead of C.

**Rows 22 and 24:** Rep Rows 2 and 4, using D instead of B.

**Row 23:** Rep Row 1, using D instead of B.

Rep Rows 1–24 for pat until throw measure approx 48 inches from beg. Change to smaller needle and work 10 rows of garter st with A. Bind off all sts. ∎

# Springtime Ripples

DESIGN BY MELISSA LEAPMAN

## EXPERIENCE LEVEL

**EASY**

## FINISHED SIZE

Approx 46 x 56 inches

## MATERIALS

- Cotton medium weight yarn (114 yds/2½ oz per ball): 7 balls light green (A); 11 balls variegated (B), 9 balls rose pink (C)
- Size 11 (8mm) circular needle
- Size 13 (9mm) circular needle or size needed to obtain gauge

## GAUGE

12 sts and 15 rows = 4 inches/10cm with larger needle and 2 strands of yarn held tog
To save time, take time to check gauge.

## STRIPE PAT

Work 10 rows A; *6 rows B, 2 rows A, 6 rows C, 2 rows A, rep from * for pat.

## PATTERN NOTES

Project uses 2 strands of yarn held tog throughout.

Circular needles are used to accommodate the large number of sts; do not join at end of rows.

## THROW

With smaller needle and 2 strands of A held tog, cast on 138 sts. Work 10 rows of garter st.

Change to larger needle and beg main pat:

**Row 1 (RS):** Knit.

**Row 2:** Purl.

**Rows 3–6:** Rep Rows 1 and 2.

**Row 7:** *[K2tog] 4 times, [yo, k1] 7 times; yo, [ssk] 4 times; rep from * across.

**Row 8:** Knit.

Rep Rows 1–8 in Stripe Pat until throw measures approx 55 inches from beg, ending with Row 6 of pat.

Change to smaller needle and A, work 10 rows of garter st. Bind off all sts. ■

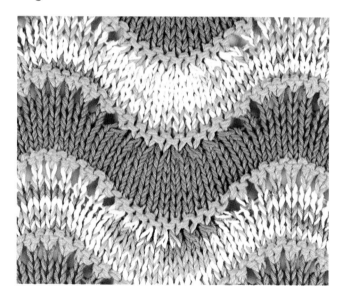

# Zigzag Eyelet Throw

DESIGN BY MELISSA LEAPMAN

## EXPERIENCE LEVEL

**EASY**

## FINISHED SIZE
Approx 40 x 50 inches

## MATERIALS

- Cotton medium weight yarn (114 yds/2½ oz per ball): 17 balls yellow
- Size 11 (8mm) circular needle
- Size 13 (9mm) circular needle or size needed to obtain gauge
- Stitch markers

## GAUGE
12 sts and 16 rows = 4 inches/10cm with larger needle and 2 strands of yarn held tog
To save time, take time to check gauge.

## PATTERN NOTES
Project uses 2 strands of yarn held tog throughout.

Circular needles are used to accommodate the large number of sts; do not join at end of rows.

## THROW
With smaller needle and 2 strands of yarn held tog, cast on 120 sts. Work 10 rows of garter st.

Change to larger needle and beg main pat:
**Row 1 (RS):** K5, place marker, k7, *k2tog, yo, k8; rep from * across to last 8 sts, end k2tog, yo, k1, place marker, K5.
**Row 2 and all WS rows:** K5, purl across to last 5 sts, k5.

**Row 3:** K11, *k2tog, yo, k8; rep from * across to last 9 sts, end k2tog, yo, k7.
**Row 5:** K10, *k2tog, yo, k8; rep from * across to last 10 sts, end k2tog, yo, k8.
**Row 7:** K9, *k2tog, yo, k8; rep from * across to last 11 sts, end k2tog, yo, k9.
**Row 9:** K8, *k2tog, yo, k8; rep from * across to last 12 sts, end k2tog, yo, k10.
**Row 11:** K7, *k2tog, yo, k8; rep from * across to last 13 sts, end k2tog, yo, k11.
**Row 13:** K6, *k2tog, yo, k8; rep from * across to last 14 sts, end k2tog, yo, k12.
**Row 15:** K5, *k2tog, yo, k8; rep from * across to last 15 sts, end k2tog, yo, k13.
**Row 17:** K7, *yo, ssk, k8; rep from * across to last 13 sts, end yo, ssk, k11.
**Row 19:** K8, *yo, ssk, k8; rep from * across to last 12 sts, end yo, ssk, k10.
**Row 21:** K9, *yo, ssk, k8; rep from * across to last 11 sts, end yo, ssk, k9.
**Row 23:** K10, *yo, ssk, k8; rep from * across to last 10 sts, end yo, ssk, k8.
**Row 25:** K11, *yo, ssk, k8; rep from * across to last 9 sts, end yo, ssk, k7.
**Row 27:** K12, *yo, ssk, k8; rep from * across to last 8 sts, end yo, ssk, k6.
**Row 29:** K13, *yo, ssk, k8; rep from * across to last 7 sts, end yo, ssk, k5.

Rep Rows 3–30 for pat until throw measures approx 49 inches from beg, ending with Row 16 of pat.

Change to smaller needle and work 10 rows of garter st. Bind off all sts. ▪

HOUSE OF WHITE BIRCHES, BERNE, INDIANA 46711   WWW.WHITEBIRCHES.COM

# Diagonal Mosaic Throw

DESIGN BY MELISSA LEAPMAN

## EXPERIENCE LEVEL

INTERMEDIATE

## FINISHED SIZE
Approx 39 x 53 inches

## MATERIALS
- Mercerized cotton worsted weight yarn (77 yds/1¾ oz per ball): 25 balls emerald (A), 19 balls lime (B)
- Size 10 (6mm) circular needle
- Size 11 (8mm) circular needle or size needed to obtain gauge

**4 MEDIUM**

## GAUGE
10 sts and 16 rows = 4 inches/10cm with larger needle and 3 strands of yarn held tog
To save time, take time to check gauge.

## PATTERN NOTES
Project uses 3 strands of yarn held tog throughout.

Circular needles are used to accommodate the large number of sts; do not join at end of rows.

Sl all sts as if to purl, holding yarn to WS of fabric (in back on knit rows, in front on purl rows).

## THROW
With smaller needles and 3 strands of A held tog, cast on 121 sts and work 10 rows of garter st.

Change to larger needle and beg main pat:

**Row 1 (RS):** With A, k5; with B, k3,*sl1 wyib, k3, rep from * across to last 5 sts; end k5 with 2nd ball of A.

**Row 2:** With A, k5; with B, p3, *sl1 wyif, p3, rep from * across to last 5 sts; end k5 with 2nd ball of A.

**Row 3:** With A, k5, *sl1 wyib, k3, rep from * across to last 8 sts, end sl1 wyib, k7.

**Row 4:** With A, k5, p2, *sl1 wyif, p3, rep from * across to last 6 sts, end sl1 wyif, k5.

**Row 5:** With A, k5; with B, k1, *sl1 wyib, k3, rep from * across to last 7 sts, end sl1 wyib, k1; k5 with 2nd ball of A.

**Row 6:** With A, k5; with B, p1, *sl1 wyif, p3, rep from * across to last 7 sts, sl1 wyif, p1; k5 with 2nd ball of A.

**Row 7:** With A, k7, *sl1 wyib, k3, rep from * across to last 6 sts, ending sl1 wyib, k5.

**Row 8:** With A, k5, *sl1 wyif, p3, rep from * across to last 8 sts, end sl1 wyif, p2, k5.

Rep Rows 1–8 for pat until throw measures approx 52 inches from beg, ending with Row 2 of pat.

Change to smaller needle and work 10 rows of garter st with A. Bind off all sts. ■

 HOUSE OF WHITE BIRCHES, BERNE, INDIANA 46711 WWW.WHITEBIRCHES.COM

# Quick Confetti Throw

DESIGN BY MELISSA LEAPMAN

## EXPERIENCE LEVEL

BEGINNER

## FINISHED SIZE

Approx 43 x 53 inches

## MATERIALS

- Cotton medium weight yarn (114 yds/2½ oz per ball): 19 balls pastel variegated
- Size 11 (8mm) circular needle
- Size 13 (9mm) circular needle or size needed to obtain gauge

## GAUGE

12 sts and 16 rows = 4 inches/10cm with larger needle and 2 strands of yarn held tog
To save time, take time to check gauge.

## PATTERN NOTES

Project uses 2 strands of yarn held tog throughout.

Circular needles are used to accommodate the large number of sts; do not join at end of rows.

## THROW

With smaller needle and 2 strands of yarn held tog, cast on 126 sts. Work 10 rows of garter st.

Change to larger needle and beg main pat:

**Row 1 (RS):** Knit across.
**Row 2:** K5, *k2tog; rep from * across to last 5 sts, end k5.
**Row 3:** K5, *knit into front and back of next st, rep from * across, end k5.
**Row 4:** K5, *purl across to last 5 sts, end k5.

Rep Rows 1–4 for pat until throw measures approx 52 inches from beg, ending with Row 4 of pat.

Change to smaller needle and work 10 rows of garter st. Bind off all sts. ■

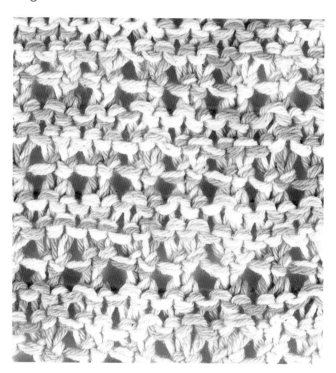

HOUSE OF WHITE BIRCHES, BERNE, INDIANA 46711   WWW.WHITEBIRCHES.COM

# Quick Patriotic Throw

DESIGN BY MELISSA LEAPMAN

## EXPERIENCE LEVEL

**INTERMEDIATE**

## FINISHED SIZE
Approx 42 x 54 inches

## MATERIALS

- Cotton medium weight yarn (114 yds/2½ oz per ball): 13 balls of deep blue (A); 5 balls each red (B), white (C)
- Size 11 (8mm) circular needle
- Size 13 (9mm) circular needle or size needed to obtain gauge

## GAUGE
12 sts and 15 rows = 4 inches/10cm with larger needle and 2 strands of yarn held tog
To save time, take time to check gauge.

## PATTERN NOTES
Project uses 2 strands of yarn held tog throughout.

Circular needles are used to accommodate the large number of sts; do not join at end of rows.

Sl all sts purlwise with yarn on WS of fabric.

## THROW
With smaller needle and 2 strands of A held tog, cast on 125 sts. Work 10 rows of garter st.

Change to larger needle and beg main pat:
**Row 1 (RS):** With A, knit.
**Row 2:** With A, k5, purl across to last 5 sts, k5.

**Row 3:** With A, k5; with B, k1, *sl 1, k3; rep from * to last 7 sts, end k1; with 2nd ball of A, k5.
**Row 4:** With A, k5; with B, p1, *sl 1, p3; rep from * to last 7 sts, end sl 1, p1; with 2nd ball of A, k5.
**Rows 5 and 6:** With A, rep Rows 1 and 2.
**Row 7:** With A, k5; with C, k3, *sl 1, k3; rep from * to last 4 sts; end k5 with 2nd ball of A.
**Row 8:** With A, k5; with C, p3, *sl 1, p3; rep from * to last 5 sts; end k5 with 2nd ball of A.

Rep Rows 1–8 for pat until throw measures approx 51 inches from beg, ending with Row 6 of pat.

Change to smaller needle and work ten rows of garter st with A. Bind off all sts. ■

# Quick Textured Afghan

DESIGN BY ANN E. SMITH

## EXPERIENCE LEVEL

**BEGINNER**

## FINISHED SIZE
Approx 43½ x 53½ inches

## MATERIALS
- Worsted weight yarn (210 yds/ 100g per skein): 15 skeins grey heather
- Size 15 (10mm) circular needle or size needed to obtain gauge

**4 MEDIUM**

## GAUGE
10 sts and 14 rows = 4 inches/10cm in body pat with 3 strands of yarn held tog
To save time, take time to check gauge.

## PATTERN NOTES
Project uses 3 strands of yarn held tog throughout.

Circular needle is used to accommodate the large number of sts; do not join at end of rows.

## AFGHAN
Beg at lower edge, cast on 113 sts.

## BORDER
**Row 1 (WS):** K6, [p4, k3] across, end p4, k5.
**Row 2:** K5, *[sl 1 purlwise, k1, yo, pass sl st over k1 and yo] twice, k3, rep from * across, end k6 instead of k3.
**Rows 3–11:** Rep Rows 1 and 2 end with Row 1.

## BODY PAT
**Row 1 (RS):** K2, p1, [k3, p1] across, end k2.
**Row 2:** P2, [k5, p3] across, end k5, p2.
**Rows 3–6:** Rep Rows 1 and 2.
**Row 7:** Rep Row 1.
**Row 8:** K3, [p3, k5] across, end p3, k3.
**Row 9:** K2, [p1, k3] across, end p1, k2.
**Rows 10 and 11:** Rep Rows 8 and 9.
**Row 12:** Rep Row 8.
**Rows 13–156:** Rep Rows 1–12.

## BORDER
Work 11 rows of border pat, beg and ending with Row 2.

Bind off all sts in pat on WS. ■

# Easy as Can Be

DESIGN BY ANN E. SMITH

## EXPERIENCE LEVEL

**BEGINNER**

## FINISHED SIZE
Approx 46 x 60 inches, excluding fringe

## MATERIALS
- Worsted weight yarn (210 yds/ 100g per skein): 8 skeins Aran (MC); 5 skeins each navy heather (A), blue heather (B), mulberry heather (C)
- Size 13 (9mm) circular needle or size needed to obtain gauge
- Crochet hook (for fringe)

## GAUGE
10½ sts = 4 inches/10cm; 40 rows/5 stripes = 8 inches/20cm in pat with 2 strands of yarn held tog
To save time, take time to check gauge.

## PATTERN NOTES
Project uses 2 strands of yarn held tog throughout.

Sl all sts purlwise with yarn on WS of fabric.

To use 5th skeins of A, B and C, wind each skein into 2 separate balls.

Circular needle is used to accommodate the large number of sts; do not join at end of rows.

## AFGHAN
Beg at lower edge with MC, cast on 125 sts.
**Rows 1–6:** With MC, knit.

**Row 7:** With A, k1, [yo, k2tog] across.
**Rows 8–14:** With A, knit.
**Rows 15–22:** With MC, rep Rows 7–14.
**Rows 23–30:** With B, rep Rows 7–14.
**Rows 31–39:** With MC, rep Rows 7–14.
**Rows 40–48:** With C, rep Rows 7–14.
**Rows 49–56:** With MC, rep Rows 7–14.
**Rows 57–306:** Rep Rows 7–56.
Loosely bind off knitwise.

## FRINGE
*Cut 6 (10-inch) strands of MC. Holding strands tog, fold in half to form lp. With WS of afghan facing, using crochet hook, pull lp through corner at lower edge; pull ends through lp and tighten to form a knot. Rep from * every 2nd or 3rd st or as desired across both ends. ∎

# Surprisingly Simple Afghan

DESIGN BY ANN E. SMITH

## EXPERIENCE LEVEL

**EASY**

## FINISHED SIZE
Approx 40 x 50 inches

## MATERIALS
- Worsted weight yarn (210 yds/100g per skein): 8 skeins mulberry heather (MC), 4 skeins winter white (CC)
- Size 13 (9mm) circular needle or size needed to obtain gauge

**4 MEDIUM**

## GAUGE
12 sts and 13 rows = 4 inches/10cm with 2 strands of yarn held tog
To save time, take time to check gauge.

## PATTERN NOTES
Project uses 2 strands of yarn held tog throughout.

Sl all sts purlwise with yarn on WS of fabric.

Circular needle is used to accommodate the large number of sts; do not join at end of rows.

## AFGHAN
Beg at lower edge with MC, cast on 119 sts.

## BORDER
**Rows 1, 3, 5 and 7 (WS):** Purl.
**Row 2:** Knit.
**Row 4:** K1, [yo, k2tog] across.
**Row 6:** Knit.

## BODY PAT
**Row 1: (RS):** With CC, knit.
**Row 2:** With CC, knit.

**Rows 3–6:** With MC, beg with a knit row, work in St st.
**Row 7:** With CC, k7, *sl 2, k1, sl 2, k5; rep from * across, end sl 2, k1, sl 2, k7.
**Row 8:** With CC, k7, *sl 2, k1, sl 2, k5; rep from * across, end sl 2, k1, sl 2. k7.
**Rows 9–12:** Rep Rows 3–6.
**Rows 13 and 14:** Rep Rows 1 and 2.
**Rows 15–18:** Rep Rows 3–6.
**Row 19:** With CC, k3, sl 3, *k3, sl 1, k3, sl 3; rep from * across, end k3.
**Row 20:** With CC, k3, sl 3, *k3, sl 1, k3, sl 3; rep from * across, end k3.
**Row 21:** With MC, knit.
**Row 22:** With MC, purl.
**Rows 23 and 24:** Rep Rows 19 and 20.
**Rows 25–28:** Rep Rows 3–6.
**Rows 29 and 30:** Rep Rows 1 and 2.
**Rows 31–34:** Rep Rows 3–6.
**Row 35:** With CC, k1, sl 1, k1, sl 3, * [k1, sl 1] 3 times, k1, sl 3; rep from * across, end last rep k1, sl 1, k1.
**Row 36:** With CC, k1, sl 1, k1, sl 3, *[k1, sl 1] 3 times, k1, sl 3; rep from * across, end last rep k1, wyif, sl 1, wyib, k1.
**Rows 37 and 38:** Rep Rows 21 and 22.
**Rows 39–46:** Rep Rows 35–38.
**Rows 47 and 48:** Rep Rows 21 and 22.
**Rows 49–222:** Rep Rows 1–48, end with Row 30.

## BORDER
**Rows 1–3:** With MC, beg with a knit row work 3 rows St st.
**Row 4 (WS):** P1, [yo, p2tog] across.
**Rows 5–7:** Beg with a knit row, work 3 rows St st. Bind off knitwise on WS of fabric.

Fold border to WS along eyelet row and whipstitch in place. Rep for opposite edge. ■

# Soft Stripes Afghan

DESIGN BY ANN E. SMITH

## EXPERIENCE LEVEL

**EASY**

## FINISHED SIZE

Approx 42 x 53 inches

## MATERIALS

- Worsted weight yarn (210 yds/ 100g per skein): 9 skeins winter white (MC); 3 skeins each dark purple (A), purple (B), light purple (C)
- Size 15 (10mm) circular needle or size needed to obtain gauge

**4 MEDIUM**

## GAUGE

10 sts and 16 rows = 4 inches/10cm in pat with 3 strands of yarn held tog
To save time, take time to check gauge.

## PATTERN NOTES

Project uses 3 strands of yarn held tog throughout.
    Sl all sts purlwise with yarn on WS of fabric.
    Circular needle is used to accommodate the large number of sts; do not join at end of rows.

## AFGHAN

Beg at lower edge with MC, cast on 105 sts.

## BORDER

**Rows 1–4:** Knit.
**Row 5:** K1, [yo, k2tog] across.
**Rows 6–9:** Knit, dec 1 st on Row 9. (104 sts)

## BODY PAT

**Row 1 (RS):** With MC, knit.

**Row 2:** With MC, purl.
**Row 3:** With A, k1, [sl 2, k2] across, end sl 2, k1.
**Row 4:** With A, p1, [sl 2, p2] across, end sl 2, p1.
**Rows 5–8:** Rep Rows 1–4.
**Row 9:** With A, knit.
**Row 10:** With A, purl.
**Row 11:** With MC, k1, [sl 2, k2] across, end sl 2, k1.
**Row 12:** With MC, p1, [sl 2, p2] across, end sl 2, p1.
**Rows 13–16:** Rep Rows 9–12.
**Row 17:** With MC, knit.
**Row 18:** With MC, purl.
**Rows 19–20:** With B, rep Rows 3 and 4.
**Rows 21–24:** Rep Rows 17–20.
**Row 25:** With B, knit.
**Row 26:** With B, purl.
**Rows 27–28:** With MC, rep Rows 11 and 12.
**Rows 29–32:** Rep Rows 25–28.
**Row 33:** With MC, knit.
**Row 34:** With MC, purl.
**Rows 35–36:** With C, rep Rows 3 and 4.
**Rows 37–40:** Rep Rows 33–36.
**Row 41:** With C, knit.
**Row 42:** With C, purl.
**Rows 43–44:** With MC, rep Rows 11 and 12.
**Rows 45–48:** Rep Rows 41–44.
**Rows 49–192:** [Rep Rows 1–48]
3 times.
**Rows 193 and 194:** Rep Rows 1 and 2.

## LOWER BORDER

**Rows 1–4:** With MC, knit, inc 1 st on Row 1. (105 sts)
**Row 5:** K1, [yo, k2tog] across.
**Rows 6–9:** Knit.
    Bind off all sts knitwise. ∎

# Hudson Bay

DESIGN BY ANN E. SMITH

## EXPERIENCE LEVEL

BEGINNER

## FINISHED SIZE
Approx 40 x 50 inches, excluding fringe

## MATERIALS
- Worsted weight yarn (210 yds/ 100g per skein): 6 skeins winter white (MC); 3 skeins each rich country blue (A), pale bronze (B), country pink (C)
- Size 15 (10mm) circular needle
- Size H (5mm) crochet hook

## GAUGE
11 sts and 20 rows = 5 inches/12.5cm in body pat with 3 strands of yarn held tog
To save time, take time to check gauge.

## PATTERN NOTES
Project uses 3 strands of yarn held tog throughout.

Circular needle is used to accommodate the large number of sts; do not join at end of rows.

## PATTERN STITCH
**Row 1 (RS):** P3, [k1, p3, k1, p6] across, end [k1, p3] twice.

**Row 2:** K3, [p1, k3, p1, k6] across, end [p1, k3] twice.

**Row 3:** Knit.

**Row 4:** K5, [p1, k10] across, end p1, k5.

**Row 5:** P5, [k1, p10] across, end k1, p5.

**Row 6:** Purl.

Rep Rows 1–6 for pat.

## AFGHAN
Beg at lower edge with MC, cast on 88 sts. Purl 1 row.

## BORDER
**Rows 1–8:** Work Rows 1–6 of pat, then rep Rows 1 and 2.

**Rows 9–17:** With A, work in established pat, ending with Row 5.

**Rows 18–26:** With MC, work in established pat, ending with Row 2.

**Rows 27–35:** With B, rep Rows 9–17.

**Rows 36–44:** With MC, rep Rows 18–26.

**Rows 45–53:** With C, rep Rows 9–17.

## BODY
With MC, beg with Row 6, work in established pat until piece measures approx 37 inches from beg, ending with Row 2.

## BORDER
**Rows 1–9:** With C, rep Rows 9–17.

**Rows 10–18:** With MC, rep Rows 18–26.

**Rows 19–27:** With B, rep Rows 9–17.

**Rows 28–36:** With MC, rep Rows 18–26.

**Rows 37–45:** With A, rep Rows 9–17.

**Rows 46–54:** With MC, rep Rows 18–26.

Loosely bind off all sts knitwise.

## FRINGE
*Cut 6 (10-inch) strands; fold in half to form lp. With WS of afghan facing, using crochet hook, pull lp through lower edge in center of knit-purl stripe. Draw ends through lp and pull snug. Rep from * across each end (16 fringes). ■

# Heather Glen

DESIGN BY ANN E. SMITH

## EXPERIENCE LEVEL

**EASY**

## FINISHED SIZE

Approx 42 x 52 inches

## MATERIALS

- Worsted weight yarn (210 yds/ 100g per skein): 10 skeins Aran (MC), 4 skeins forest heather (A), 2 skeins pale forest heather (B)
- Size 13 (9mm) circular needle or size needed to obtain gauge

**4 MEDIUM**

## GAUGE

12 sts = 4 inches/10cm in pat with 2 strands of yarn held tog
To save time, take time to check gauge

## PATTERN NOTES

Project uses 2 strands of yarn held tog throughout.

Sl all sts purlwise with yarn on WS of fabric.

Circular needle is used to accommodate the large number of sts; do not join at end of rows.

## BODY PATTERN

**Row 1 (RS):** K2, [sl 1, k1] across, end last rep sl 1, k2.
**Row 2:** P1, [k1, p1] across.
**Row 3:** K1, [sl 1, k1] across.
**Row 4:** K1, [p1, k1] across.
Rep Rows 1–4 for pat.

## AFGHAN

Beg at lower edge with A, cast on 125 sts.

## BORDER

**Rows 1–12:** With A, rep Rows 1–4.

**Rows 13–16:** With MC, rep Rows 1–4.
**Rows 17–28:** With B, rep Rows 1–4.
**Rows 29–32:** With MC, rep Rows 1–4.
**Rows 33–44:** With A, rep Rows 1–4.
**Rows 45–56:** With MC, rep Rows 1–4.

## BOX PATTERN

**Row 1 (RS):** With B, k4, sl 1, [k3, sl 1] across, end k4.
**Row 2:** With B, k4, sl 1, [k3, sl 1] across, end k4.
**Row 3:** With MC, k1, [sl 1, k1] across.
**Row 4:** With MC, k1, [sl 1, k1] across.
**Rows 5–8:** Rep Rows 1–4.
**Rows 9–20:** With MC, rep border Rows 1–12.
**Rows 21–28:** With A, rep box pat Rows 1–8.
**Rows 29–40:** With MC, rep border Rows 1–12.
**Rows 41–48:** With B, rep box pat Rows 1–8.

## AFGHAN BODY

With MC, rep body pat Rows 1–4 until piece measures approx 36½ inches from beg, ending with Row 4.

Rep box pat Rows 1–48.

## BORDER

**Rows 1–12:** With MC, rep border Rows 45–56.
**Rows 13–56:** Rep border Rows 1–44.
With A, loosely bind off knitwise. ■

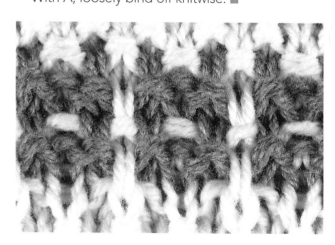

HOUSE OF WHITE BIRCHES, BERNE, INDIANA 46711 WWW.WHITEBIRCHES.COM

# Sherbet Ripple

DESIGN BY ANN E. SMITH

## EXPERIENCE LEVEL

**EASY**

## FINISHED SIZE
Approx 42 x 57 inches

## MATERIALS
- Worsted weight yarn (210yds/ 100g per skein): 6 skeins pale aqua (A); 4 skeins each periwinkle (B), pale periwinkle (C); 3 skeins each aqua (D), winter white (E)
- Size 15 (10mm) circular needle or size needed to obtain gauge

**4 MEDIUM**

## GAUGE
10 sts and 14 rows = 4 inches/10cm in body pat with 3 strands of yarn held tog
To save time, take time to check gauge.

## PATTERN NOTES
Project uses 3 strands of yarn held tog throughout.

To use 4th skeins of B and C, wind each skein into 3 separate balls.

Circular needle is used to accommodate the large number of sts; do not join at end of rows.

## AFGHAN
Beg at lower edge with D, cast on 105 sts.

## BORDER
**Row 1 (WS):** Knit.
**Row 2:** K2, p101, k2.
**Row 3:** Knit.
**Rows 4 and 5:** Rep Rows 2 and 3. Cut D.

## BODY PATTERN
**Row 1 (RS):** With A, k4, yo, k5, k3tog, k5, yo, *k1, yo, k5; k3tog, k5, yo, rep from * across, end k4.

**Row 2:** K2, p101, k2.
**Row 3:** Knit.
**Row 4:** Rep Row 1.
**Rows 5–8:** Rep Rows 1–4.
**Rows 9–11:** Rep Rows 1–3.
**Row 12 (WS):** With B, k2, p101, k2.
**Row 13:** Rep Row 12.
**Row 14:** Knit.
**Row 15:** Rep Row 12.
**Row 16:** Knit
**Rows 17–27:** With C, rep Rows 1–11.
**Rows 28–32:** With E, rep Rows 12–16.
**Rows 33–43:** With A, rep Rows 1–11.
**Rows 44–48:** With E, rep Rows 12–16.
**Rows 49–59:** With B, rep Rows 1–11.
**Rows 60–64:** With D, rep Rows 12–16.
**Rows 65–176:** Rep Rows 1–64 in color sequence as given, ending with Row 48.
**Rows 177–187:** With C, rep Rows 1–11.
**Rows 188–192:** With B, rep Rows 12–16.
**Rows 193–203:** With A, rep Rows 1–11.
**Rows 204–208:** With D, rep Rows 12–16.
With D, loosely bind off knitwise. ■

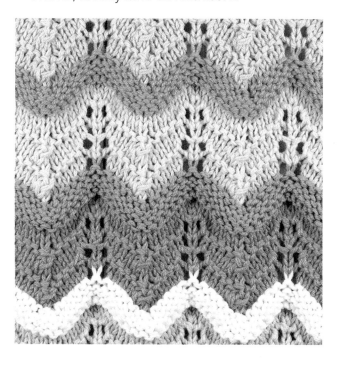

HOUSE OF WHITE BIRCHES, BERNE, INDIANA 46711  WWW.WHITEBIRCHES.COM

# Standard Abbreviations

[ ] work instructions within brackets as many times as directed

( ) work instructions within parentheses in the place directed

** repeat instructions following the asterisks as directed

* repeat instructions following the single asterisk as directed

" inch(es)

**approx** approximately

**beg** begin/beginning

**CC** contrasting color

**ch** chain stitch

**cm** centimeter(s)

**cn** cable needle

**dec** decrease/decreases/ decreasing

**dpn(s)** double-pointed needle(s)

**g** gram

**inc** increase/increases/ increasing

**k** knit

**k2tog** knit 2 stitches together

**LH** left hand

**lp(s)** loop(s)

**m** meter(s)

**M1** make one stitch

**MC** main color

**mm** millimeter(s)

**oz** ounce(s)

**p** purl

**pat(s)** pattern(s)

**p2tog** purl 2 stitches together

**psso** pass slipped stitch over

**rem** remain/remaining

**rep** repeat(s)

**rev St st** reverse stockinette stitch

**RH** right hand

**rnd(s)** rounds

**RS** right side

**skp** slip, knit, pass stitch over—1 stitch decreased

**sk2p** slip 1, knit 2 together, pass slip stitch over the knit 2 together; 2 stitches have been decreased

**sl** slip

**sl 1k** slip 1 knitwise

**sl 1p** slip 1 purlwise

**sl st** slip stitch(es)

**ssk** slip, slip, knit these 2 stitches together—a decrease

**st(s)** stitch(es)

**St st** stockinette stitch/ stocking stitch

**tbl** through back loop(s)

**tog** together

**WS** wrong side

**wyib** with yarn in back

**wyif** with yarn in front

**yd(s)** yard(s)

**yfwd** yarn forward

**yo** yarn over

# Skill Levels

**BEGINNER**

Projects for first-time knitters using basic knit and purl stitches. Minimal shaping.

**EASY**

Projects using basic stitches, repetitive stitch patterns, simple color changes and simple shaping and finishing.

**INTERMEDIATE**

Projects with a variety of stitches, such as basic cables and lace, simple intarsia, double-pointed needles and knitting in the round needle techniques, mid-level shaping and finishing.

**EXPERIENCED**

Projects using advanced techniques and stitches, such as short rows, Fair Isle, more intricate intarsia, cables, lace patterns and numerous color changes.

**HOUSE of WHITE BIRCHES**
PUBLISHERS SINCE 1947

***Big Needle Afghans & Throws*** is published by House of White Birches/DRG Publishing, 306 East Parr Road, Berne, IN 46711, telephone (260) 589-4000. Printed in USA. Copyright © 2006 House of White Birches/DRG Publishing.

RETAIL STORES: If you would like to carry this pattern book or any other DRG publications, call the Wholesale Department to set up a direct account: (903) 636-4303. Also, request a complete listing of publications available.

Editor: Jeanne Stauffer
Associate Editor: Dianne Schmidt
Art Director: Brad Snow
Assistant Art Director: Nick Pierce
Technical Editor: E. J. Slayton
Copy Supervisor: Michelle Beck
Copy Editor: Mary O'Donnell
Graphic Production Supervisor: Ronda Bechinski

Graphic Artist: Nicole Gage
Photography: Tammy Christian, Don Clark, Christena Green, Matthew Owen
Photo Stylists: Tammy Nussbaum, Tammy M. Smith

Every effort has been made to ensure that the instructions in this pattern book are complete and accurate. We cannot, however, take responsibility for human error, typographical mistakes or variations in individual work.

ISBN: 978-1-59217-111-8     Printed in U.S.A.     3 4 5 6 7 8 9